Images of Me

The Images of Me

Tamara McKnight

THE IMAGES OF ME
Published by Purposely Created Publishing Group™

Copyright © 2016 Tamara McKnight

ALL RIGHTS RESERVED.

No part of this book may be reproduced, distributed or transmitted in any form by any means, graphics, electronics, or mechanical, including photocopy, recording, taping, or by any information storage or retrieval system, without permission in writing from the publisher, except in the case of reprints in the context of reviews, quotes, or references.

Scriptures marked ESV are taken from Holy Bible, *English Standard Version®*. Copyright © 2001 by Crossway, a publishing ministry of Good News Publishers. All rights reserved.

Scriptures marked NIV are taken from the Holy Bible, *New International Version®*, NIV®. Copyright © 1973, 1978, 1984, 2011 by Biblica, Inc.™. All rights reserved.

Printed in the United States of America

ISBN (ebook): 978-1-945558-04-7
ISBN (paperback): 978-1-945558-03-0

Special discounts are available on bulk quantity purchases by book clubs, associations and special interest groups. For details email: sales@publishyourgift.com
or call (888) 949-6228.

For information logon to:
www.PublishYourGift.com

Dedication

This book is dedicated to all the survivors of child molestation and all forms of sexual assault. I pray that you find peace after reading this as I did after writing it. Allow God to work in your life, for him to bring you out of your darkness. If you can push yourself to be better, you will see that it was all worth it in the end. I am so thankful for my trials and tribulations because they made me a stronger, better woman.

Table of Contents

Dedication	v
Acknowledgments	ix
Introduction	1
The Images of Me	5
Moving Time	10
Weekend Getaways	13
Real Life Beginnings	21
Let's Give It Another Try	33
Let the Fun Begin	37
Motherhood	41
Let's Try Dating Again	45
Opening Up and Letting Go	49
Peace and Blessings	
How to Heal	57
Beautiful You Are	58

Self-Love/Love Thyself	59
Know Your Worth	60
Peace of Mind	61
Purpose	62
Truth Be Told	63
Afraid to Love	64
Imperfect You	65
You Are Queens	66
Forgiveness	67
Determination	68
About the Author	69

Acknowledgments

First I want to thank my Lord and Savior, Jesus Christ, for bringing me this far. Who ever knew that this young black girl could write a book? But with prayer, anything is possible. Thank you Lord for blessing me with my son Jadon Wilson. He is the best gift I could ever ask for. When I told God I wanted a boy, who would have ever thought he would bless me with him? He is my world and my sunshine on my darkest days. He unconditionally loves me, and I love him.

To my mother, I know raising four girls was a challenge for you, and we gave you a hard way to go, but with the grace of God, we all made it. You will forever be my old lady. I will always be there by your side. Our past is our past. God kept us around to make our future brighter. With you by my side, it will be great.

To my three beautiful sisters, I know I am the mother for real, and I get on all of y'all nerves—just know I want all of us to be great. I did not just write the book for me, I wrote it for us. We are a family, so my success will shine through all of us. I love you all with all my heart.

To my Aunt Brenda, my second mother, I could not imagine life without you. You helped my mom for so many years, raising me to be the strong woman I am today, and I will forever be grateful. You were always the woman I could run to for advice or just a listening ear, and I thank you for helping me.

To my best friends that stuck with me through thick and thin, I share this book with you as well. We have had our difficulties, but we made it work. I love you all so much.

To Tynisha Hall, the best of the best, you are my best friend that I look up to. I want to be strong and determined just like you. I had to do a lot of praying to get there, but you had my back through it all, and I thank God he placed you in my life. You were the first person I told my story to, and the minute you heard it, you knew it was time for me to get help. You never judged me, and I am grateful to call you my friend. Thank you for being an inspiration in my life.

To all my family, I love y'all dearly. To my friends that I met along this journey, thank you for just being so kind to me. Most of all, to my Med Surg 2 pavilion work family, thank you for accepting me, and I love working with y'all every day. Love you guys.

Last but not least, my sis in Christ, my mentor, Angela D. Wharton, you are truly an amazing woman. Meeting you was the best part of my life. If it were not for you and Phynyx Ministries, I would have never written this book. During the storm that I was going through for two years, you were right there with me, praying for me in the middle of your workday, which got me through my day. I know I could not have done this book without you. Thank you so much, and I love you dearly.

Now I'm just ready to change the world.

Peace and Blessings

Introduction

This is a book full of a young girl's pain and triumph, from the hood (ghetto), who grew up into a beautiful, strong woman. Let me take you on a tour of me, starting you off with pain and ending with healing, with the mercy and grace from God that brought me through it all.

Prayer was the only thing that pulled me through. He saved me so I could help save someone like me. At the end of this book, I give you daily quotes and encouragements you can read to get you through your good days or bad days, but mainly those bad days. I pray that this book helps you with the journey you have set yourself on. It sure was not easy for me, but we all have a testimony that has to be shared to help one another. I will take you on a little tour of growing up, from being molested as a child to watching physical abuse go on in my home, to just growing up with hate in my heart. A child that endured so much but overcame everything that the devil stole from her.

My mentor once told me, you will write a book one day. She was telling me something that God told her, so I had to believe every word she said.

She told me she did not know when I was going to begin this book. It was up to me to find myself and the time to start. Doubting myself, I was confused and puzzled. Where would I begin? How would it start? What would be the title? The most important question of all was, what would I talk about? Am I good enough to write this book? Would anybody buy a copy? Nobody wants a boring book to read. So many negative thoughts were roaming through my head.

I lived with negativity for the majority of my life. For many years, I never knew how to shake it off. It followed me everywhere that I went; it ruled my life. I am writing a memoir to finally release the pain and triumphs that kept me bonded for so long. A glimpse inside the world of me. It might not seem important to many, but some will understand the life that I endured. There were good times and many bad times. The thing people say about that is, "Thank God I don't look like what I've been through." Lord knows, if that was not the best quote you ever heard in your life. If you could see the scars of my past on me physically, you would probably say, girl, what have you been through? I didn't know how people would react to it. Most of my childhood is a blur. I blocked out a lot of it because it was not that great for me, so I am writing this about the major things that I remember, some of which are the negative parts. With that being said, I give you a peek into my life. This is where *The Images of Me* takes its place in life. Enjoy this read.

Tamara

Healing

Love Thyself

Beautiful You Are

Know Your Worth

The Images of Me -----

From what I can remember, growing up in this world was not as easy as most people would think. Growing up in the hood, the tough times of just living day to day took a toll on me very early on. I know you're probably like, she was only five, but guess what? It wasn't easy. I may have looked five, but my mind was always trying to find ways to escape the place I was in or the madness that surrounded me at that time--from just growing up not having much to being molested as a young child. On top of that, I watched my mom go through domestic violence and not even leave the man that was causing her pain. Hell, causing *me* pain, watching her suffer from it. I was just trying to block all the negativity that crossed my mind at the time, basically being forced to grow up so fast was all that I was faced with.

No one knew what I was going through. This could not be my childhood; it just could not be real life. There were times where I woke up not knowing what I was going to eat for breakfast or what I was going to wear to school. The dreams of being a pediatrician were starting to fade away day by day, just no hope to look for. I never really thought I would become anything as time went on, coming from a broken home where your dad got high on drugs and your mom had four children-- girls to be exact. Not getting the attention that you were supposed to get from either parent. I knew my mom and dad loved me, but I just did not feel it at times.

All I did was crave for my dad's attention. He was not around much; either he was in or out of the house running the streets or he was in and out of prison. What did he love more, his kids or the habit? At the time, I didn't know how bad the drug habit was. All I knew was that I wanted my dad at home. I wanted the family that every little girl deserves. However, that was not going on in my house. Me being the daddy's girl that I was, I could never stay mad at him.

I strongly believe that every girl needs their dad to teach them how to become queens. Nevertheless, I had to learn on my own. Trying to learn how to grow up was the hardest. Who was going to teach me about boys? Who was going to teach me how to be strong when the boys did not like me? Maybe they think I am a little ugly duckling or something along that line. Yes, I lacked confidence starting at an early age, and you might still lack it in your adulthood if your dad was not around to tell you how pretty you are or just to help you out day to day. My dad loved his girls, no question about that, but did he really know how to be a father? Too many times, he just let the streets consume his mind, body, and soul. He just kept leaving over and over again, leaving three beautiful daughters in the hands of their mother to solely take care of them on her own. If I could have gotten a job, I really would have. Sounds crazy right, but I wanted to help out with our living situation so that my mom wouldn't have to do it by herself. Dream big, little girl, one day you will go far. Yet another thought that kept playing over and over in my head.

Every girl deserves to dream big and feel happy on the inside, but darkness was all that I was feeling from time to time. Someone wake me up from this dream (or should I say nightmare?). Take me to that place where I am happy and smiling. Take me to that place where there is no more pain. That was all I could think about. Free me of burdens. It is funny because I was so young with grown-up thoughts. I love my mom and wouldn't trade her for the world, but Lord knows, it was hard for her. I grew up in a house where no one said "I love you." I guess we just hoped that it was all love. Sounds bad, but it was just my reality. Something like a bad dream, but it was my reality. Something like a sad dream, but I am thankful to this day.

I used to wake up as an angry little girl with so much hate in the inside, sometimes not even knowing why I felt that way at a young age. Some days I would sit in my room and just write on anything I could find, saying I hated everybody, questioning myself on why my mom would have so many kids without being able to really take care of them. Talking back to her was my norm. Sometimes my respect for her went out the window. Being so angry on the inside, just mad, made me be so angry with her. Angry was my middle name, and I don't think anyone could change that at the time. I was told too often that I was so hateful. I really did not care or pay it any mind. How could I let those words hurt me when they were so true at an early age?

Moving Time ----------

It's moving time again--something that happened every so often and more than the usual family. Moving from house to house, to different neighborhoods and schools, my brain was all over the place. Why couldn't we just live in a big family-size home and never have to move? But the way government assistance was created back then didn't allow you to settle in one home too long—at least I thought.

We changed schools for many years. I felt like a genie. Going to school was okay, but I was not too excited about it. I could have done much better, but not being able to truly focus in class was the hard part. My mind wandered all over the place. I found myself crying at times in class because I missed my dad. Oh, I was angry and mean to other kids as well. I once got into trouble because I cut up this little girl's eyeglass case. She was prettier than I was, so I was jealous of her. Do not forget I lacked confidence. At the time, I did not know anything about bullying, but now I guess I could say at times I was something like one. Looking back on it, I wish I never did anything like that. Never would I want anyone picking on my son.

The Images of Me

My teacher started to wonder what was going on with me. She told me it was time to call my mom. Knowing that I wasn't going to get into any trouble with my mom, it didn't bother me one bit. My teacher said, You're too young to have such a big attitude, where is it coming from? Little did she know so much trouble was going on in my household that the only place to release it was school. So my teacher found a big sister program that my mom put me and my sister into. At first I wasn't so stoked about it, but as time went on, it seemed to get better. It wasn't such a bad idea to have some other people to look out for me.

The sisters that chose me and my sister were twins. I really didn't know what to expect with them. It could be a ton of fun or it could turn out to be a big disaster. All work and no play were what the sisters were all about. I was not happy about that at all, but the great part about it was that I was really struggling with my schoolwork, and they were right there to assist us with it. To this day I greatly appreciate what they did. Once the studying was over, they would take us to have fun and meet their family, and the family loved us instantly. They were so welcoming and loved us like their own. After we had been in the program for two years, it came to an end due to low funding in the school. It was sad because I really did get attached to them and always wanted to go around them. Eventually, we all lost contact with them, but one day I will visit their church and surprise them with the success that I have accomplished. Their influence on me helped me become so much better in life, as far as being so much better in school. One thing about them, they kept God first.

Weekend Getaways

At the age of eight, all I wanted to do was sing. Sing a song and make everything go away. I'd fall so far into the music to escape from it all. Thank God for my aunt and grandmother. Those women were the saviors of the day--of my lifetime, I should say. Grandma would pick us up and take us over to her house for the weekend, the best time a little girl could ask for. All the food and snacks in the world. At home, that was just my fantasy, but I lived it out over at her house on the weekends. Might not seem like much to you, but child, it was heaven for me and my sisters. She truly loved her grandkids, and we truly loved her. I miss her to this day. A strong black queen in my eyes. She did everything that she was supposed to do as a mom and grandmother. She sacrificed many things for her kids and us.

I could be sick at home in my bed, but when the weekend came, she would still wrap me up and take me with her and my sisters just to nurse me back to health. The life of a grandma is amazing. The weekends always went pretty fast, and the thought of going back home would make me angry. At least we could take all the food and snacks that were left over back with us.

The Images of Me

One weekend was not so amazing; who would have ever thought bad things would start happening? My grandmother had a boyfriend who would come with her to pick us up. My aunt and dad called him their father. I never knew where he came from or how she really met him. He was the ride to the happy place on the weekends, so I was always extremely excited. "Heyyyy Mr. H" is what I called him. I was always excited about seeing him. Mr. H made us feel welcome, like he was our very own grandfather. He always made sure we laughed and smiled when he came around. Until one day when my smile turned into a frown.

One thing Mr. H liked to do was give us piggyback rides. What child don't like piggyback rides? My grandmother would always say to get down off of his back. Not sure on why she told me that, but she always did. Me being the sassy little girl, I would yell out, well he's my granddad, and it's fun. Little did I know at the time, I wish I would have stayed off of his back. Mr. H liked to see me do different things like flip on the bed all kinds of ways. He would stand behind the TV and cheer me on. I had no clue of the things he was doing back there at the time, but knowing now makes my stomach turn. This man would masturbate while I flipped on the bed. At the time, I couldn't figure out why his pants were always unbuttoned every time he would come from behind there. As a child, you see things, but you just don't say anything to anyone.

Things got a little crazier with him, and as I got more piggyback rides, the molesting began. Something so harmless became so bad. I was innocent, not a grown up. I was an eight-year-old, scrawny, petite, just plain ole skin and bones. Did that just happen to me? Did this man just insert his finger into my vagina? Why is he doing this to me? Should I tell? But I don't want to get him in trouble, is what I thought. I was scared. I was sick. But I wouldn't say anything to anyone. I didn't want everybody to be mad at me. Did it happen more than once? Yes. The moving of my panties to the side, over and over again, was starting to become his pattern. Please stop, you're hurting me, is all I could utter to him. Shhh, is what he told me, and that I better not tell anybody or I could never come over to my grandmother's house again. I didn't want that to happen because I loved going over there. He was the adult, and I was the child, so I had to listen.

No one knew what was going on because I was holding on to this secret. Feeling so ashamed, I kept questioning my young self. Did I do too many flips or smile too much at him for him to touch me in a way he was not supposed to? Was I too nice to him? Why did he take so much liking to me? One day, back at my grandmother's house, he invited me into the bathroom with him. I didn't want to go, but I felt like I had no choice. I didn't know what was about to happen, but he tried to insert his penis into my vagina. I yelled, Ouch, it hurts! I want out. He immediately let me go, and I ran out of that bathroom. As a child, an adult has more control over your mind than people really think. At that age, you don't think on your own. The adults think for you. But why could no one figure out what he was doing to me? Under the covers I went, feeling so ashamed and embarrassed, as I cried silently to myself so no one would hear me. That's when my life growing up changed drastically.

What I know now, and what I wish I knew back then, was to listen to grandma and stay off his back. The self-blame followed me throughout my days. Being molested can be one of the most traumatizing experiences that any child can go through, and I would never want children to ever have to go through this. He was a sick human being. To prey on innocent little girls is very sick. He made me feel so dirty inside. Just bawling, in tears every day, I grew even angrier. No one knew what was going on with me; they thought I was being my normal, mean self, and that was not the case at all. The thought of a man's hands touching me and trying to insert his penis drove me crazy. I didn't even want a man trying to give me a hug. That's when the trusting of men ended. Never would I have ever thought things like this would ever happen to me.

The hating of myself really began. Who could take advantage of a child's innocence? A man that was close to my family sure could. He took everything from me. I never allowed him to touch me again, but he also acted like nothing ever happened, and so did I. Being a kid made me block a lot of negativity out. Being sexually abused would play a huge roll in my life from then on. I didn't know it at the time, but I know now. I wanted to tell someone so bad, but I just couldn't utter the words. The hardest part of it all was wondering if someone was going to believe me or not. Everybody knew something was wrong because I kept getting asked what was wrong with me. My only reply was that I was okay.

It was time to find an escape from this world. Tuning everyone out, I buried myself in my thoughts with music and writing. At a young age, I wrote songs and poems, but never stayed consistent with it. God was preparing me then for what I am, and have begun to do, now. Music took me to a place where I felt free from the world. Such an old soul at a young age. I felt empty, and the music made me feel whole. Tears and sadness took over me. What is depression at the age of nine? I did not know, but I sure felt low. I felt hurt and pain for a long time, always asking, why me?; but getting no answers. Maybe I am just too young to understand. Maybe this happens to every little girl. Life was not fair, and I did not like it. Maybe if I just disappeared, nobody would care or miss me. I wanted to run away all the time, but I never had the courage to do so. Just make me an adult so I can just be on my own. Someone turn my mind off because I am too young to think so much and have so much pain. If only someone knew my pain and how I was feeling. Only if he never touched me, I would never be going through any of this. So many thoughts at one time. It was just so inappropriate; it just wasn't right.

The weekends at grandma's house never stopped, but the molesting did. I was still happy to go over to grandma's house to have fun and eat everything that I wanted. The pain never stopped though. I was hurting on the inside. I was sad and angry all the time, but I could not show it or tell anyone. Overall I did not want to tell just so she would not stop us from coming over. My dad started to come over to my grandmother's house, and I could not even tell him, knowing that he would go so crazy on him, and I did not want anyone to get hurt. I could not be the blame at all, so I never told.

As time went on, so did I. Growing up day by day was not easy at all. My dad was lost; he was in jail. I called jail "lost" because once you're in, you're lost to society. I am sure he felt like a lost man in there; not being around his kids and family all the time should have driven him crazy. It sure made me crazy not being able to see him when I wanted. But did he really feel that? That place was his second home. He kept going back and forth as if it was such a marvelous place to be. He was a grown man who made his own decisions. He kept messing up in life so he had to deal with the bad consequences. That did not stop me from loving him though.

Even with him behind bars, I was still daddy's little girl. My grandmother took us to see him sometimes. Those rides in the vans that picked us up at the Baltimore Arena felt so long. It was as if we were taking a trip that would never end. Once we got there, we walked through gates that look like jail bars, and the sound of the bars were mind-blowing because it felt as if we were going to be stuck in there with the inmates. All I kept saying was that I did not want to go in, but I knew that was the only way I was going to see my dad until he was released. When he did come home, I prayed he never went back.

Well I guess my prayers came true because one day he came home, and he never went back. My heart was so happy, but I still felt so sad. He might not have gone back to jail again, but he was still lost in the streets. The streets took him over: drugs, stealing, and whatever else he could get his hands on. Why oh why, I asked myself, why can't he just be normal? Normal enough to take care of his three beautiful daughters. Maybe we were not good enough for him, I thought, or maybe he just does not like us. So many negative thoughts just kept running through my head. I knew deep down that he loved us, but his bad habits took over him. Neither his kids nor anyone else could put a stop to it. That is when I had enough; I decided that if he went to jail again I was not going to see him at all. I had to save the rest of my feelings that I had left. He would just have to suffer just as if he left his daughters to do without him in our lives.

Real Life Beginnings --

Trying to enjoy everyday living is what I was doing. Once I became a teenager things seemed to become a little better, or at least I thought. I hung outside the most, me liking boys but still afraid of them. Never was I the fast girl, but I sure did like a few at a time. Was I wrong for that or was it normal? I could remember never wanting to be home or live there. I always wanted to live with other family members, but my dad was not having it. I was like, how can he get a say so in who I stay with when he is barely around? Even though I was angry, I still had to listen to him. I thought I was so grown at the age of fourteen. This one time, I decided to sit on a guy's lap and got caught by my cousin. Oh boy, did he tell the only person that put fear in me, which was my Aunt Brenda. Of course I was in trouble with her. If anything, she stayed on our backs as much as she could to keep us ladies young as long as possible.

When you're in the eleventh grade, you can't really say much, but at this point you think you're grown. Being in the eleventh grade was a challenge. I learned how to style myself a little better and do my own hair. Never could afford to go to a hair stylist. Giving a little care to what I looked like even though I didn't think I was pretty. Some boys did like me, but I just thought they wanted one thing for sure. I was still a virgin at the age of sixteen. Thank goodness for that because I sure didn't want any kids at an early age.

Helping raise my sisters was almost the worst experience I could have endured. I didn't have time to be a kid at all. Growing up so fast is what I had no choice of doing. Well suck it, you little girl, because no one wants to hear you complain about anything, is what I told myself over and over. Talking to myself was normal. No, I wasn't crazy, but that was the only thing that helped me get through my darkest days. Some days I did think I was going crazy, so many thoughts and secrets locked away in my chamber of thoughts. Days when I just wanted to turn my thoughts off with a switch, but of course that's impossible for anyone.

Just then, when I thought things couldn't get any worse for me, they did. The dad that I used to love so much died. I will never forget that day or moment. It was a summer night, and I was just outside of the house having too much fun, enjoying myself with friends, when I noticed my family approaching my house. At that moment my heart dropped. I knew something was wrong, I just didn't know what could have happened. As I walked toward the house, my stomach was in knots. I went into the house, and everybody was quiet, so I asked them what was wrong. My grandmother was the first person that spoke up. I would never forget the words that came out of her mouth: Ya he's gone. Well who's gone? is what I asked. Your father died tonight. He went into cardiac arrest and passed away. My life at that point seemed to take a pause. I felt like my life was over. Never experiencing death in my family since I was born and now the greatest person in the world to me is gone. What am I going to do? How am I going to go on with my own life? Not knowing how to feel, I couldn't even cry at the moment because I was being strong for everybody else. Why didn't I ever take the time to go see him in the rehab place? He was there for a while, and I was too selfish to go see him. Now I will never see him again. My selfishness and the thought of him not seeing me grow up didn't allow me to go and visit him. (At this moment, writing this part of the book brings back so many memories, and I'm still letting go of all that pain.) I can't think like this right now. My one and only first love is gone; I had to find a way to forgive him in my heart. It might not happen right away, but one day I will.

Preparing for the funeral was so hard. Trying to be strong for my sisters was so hard. Can you just get out of that casket, and we can just start all over with life? No drugs, no alcohol, just you and us. No more pain, I just couldn't endure anymore. Sitting by the casket I just stared at him. Maybe if I looked long enough he would just get up.

The strongest person that held it to the end was my grandmother. She was our backbone. Her breaking down when it was time to close the casket was one of the hardest things I could have witnessed. Burying my dad was hard as well, but it had to be done. God took him home, and now he is the angel of my life. (If you're reading this, honor your mother and father each and every day, and once they are gone, there's no coming back until you meet them in heaven.)

I was only sixteen. What was I going to do without my dad? Because real life was about to begin. Who would I turn to when I needed fatherly advice? My mom couldn't school me about boys or men. I don't think anyone ever taught her about them either. I was almost an adult, but I was still young at heart. I didn't have the knowledge to know that real life was going to take me on a rollercoaster ride. I asked myself, am I ready?, or will I fall victim to life and not get back up? I didn't know at that point; only the future knew what lay ahead of me. I was afraid because I lived in fear. To keep going is what I had to do for myself, in my father's memory.

When real life began, I was so not ready, but I had no choice in the matter. I was still living so I had to keep going on with it, no matter if it kept bringing me pain. I just kept through it all in hopes that one day I would see why God chose me.

It was that time—time to lose my virginity. Something that was supposed to be so special turned out not to be so great at all. Did I really know this man that was going to take something from me that's suppose to be saved for my husband on my wedding day? Or was it taken a long time ago when I got molested? The innocence is lost. That's how I felt when I gave it away. I just wanted to be loved and liked by him. Giving it away was hard, yet so easy. So why did I do it? Why did I let this man use me to get what he wanted? Why did I let him say all the right things to me to have something so sacred be taken away from me? Once it happens you can never get it back. Laying there not knowing what to do or expect, I had so many emotions. I wanted to cry; just the thought of it all made me cringe. I thought my way all through the thirty minutes or however long it lasted. I just wanted this person off of me. He didn't even know I felt that way. He wasn't taking advantage of me because I told him it was okay. It's just I really wasn't ready, but I gave it away anyway. When it was all done I felt so bad. Everything was hurting. I won't be doing that again, is what I kept telling myself.

Being so traumatized at a young age stayed with me as I got older, and I really couldn't trust men. Those feelings of being taken advantage of stayed with me when it was time to have sex with any man. This man wanted something from me that I couldn't keep giving him. He called me so much, and I never answered. It wasn't right for me to ignore him, but I couldn't help it. I didn't know what to do. I was so emotionally distressed. I felt so bad inside so I stayed away so that I couldn't be angry with him. My attitude and the nervousness stayed with me from when I was a child. The feeling of love was too painful. I didn't want to keep going on with love. I was just ready to give it up.

Three years passed, and I thought I was ready to fall in love again. Or at least I hoped I was ready. Wouldn't really know until it happened. I thought, hopefully this guy will be my everything. (Pause) This is where it started. Me looking for love and rushing into things instead of love finding me and taking things slow. Ha, slow was not in my mindset at all. Moving fast was all I knew. Well there he was, light skin, so handsome, well dressed, and we grew up around the same people. We met at a party in the same neighborhood we grew up in. Seeing him across the room, it felt like a match made in heaven. He stared at me like he had known me forever, or maybe it was just something he wanted. By the end of the night we were talking. When the party was over he kindly walked me halfway home. He was so nice to me, and I couldn't help but smile at him. Giving him my number felt so right, and we started talking on the phone that night. Back then it was only talking on the phone and no texting. And that's when the relationship began between me and him.

When it was time for the important stuff to happen (sex), of course I was scared. He made things feel so comfortable, and it made my nervousness go away. All I kept saying to myself was, he is the one, he might be my forever, or at least I thought. At least he made me feel special and wanted. He was my everything at the time. Puppy love they called it, since I was only nineteen. But to me it felt like real love. A couple of forevers. Even though I always felt like I was too mature for him, I still stayed in the relationship. The relationship was okay, could have been better, but what did I expect at such a young age? The thing we did most was argue. Boy, I tell you, he was so argumentative. The arguing got so bad I started to have anxiety. Every time we would get into an argument, my heart would race so bad that I thought I was having a heart attack. That's the part of the relationship that I hated.

The most amazing thing he did for me was pay for my trip to Disney World with him and his family. That was the most amazing experience I had had in my life. It made me fall so deeply in love with him. Sometimes things seemed too good to be true. I've always had that woman's intuition about things going on around me, and I felt it when it was time to leave for the trip. We were waiting to board the bus for the sixteen-hour drive to Florida. That's when I spotted this girl that was prettier than me. (Yes, the low self-esteem stuck with me for many years.) She looked over at us, and I couldn't figure out why, or did she know him? That was the girl he was going to cheat on me with. I thought about it, and maybe I spoke it into existence, but my intuition was telling me she was not right, and soon he was not going to be right either.

On with this trip, because the fun never stopped until one of the days on the trip he wanted to pick an argument with me, and I couldn't figure out why. The things he started to say were so hurtful. Maybe he met up with that girl I spotted, because things were too strange. All I'm thinking about at this point was when I got home, this relationship was going to be over. I didn't know where all this came from, or what was really going on, but in due time I was to find out.

The trip ended, and it was time to go home. I couldn't be happier. Yet another failed relationship. At least it lasted for a year. That sixteen-hour ride home was silent for me. I didn't want to talk to anybody. How could he ruin my trip like that? His selfishness was the most disrespectful thing I had ever seen. Never again will I go with him anywhere. He tried to be nice to me on the ride back home, but I was not having it.

We lived three blocks from each other, so one day when he wasn't answering the phone, I decided to take a visit around his house. I just knew something was going on. When I knocked on the front door, his mom answered. She let me know he was upstairs and gave me the key to his room. She knew what was going on so she let me handle it. I crept up the steps and hurried up and opened the door. I was in shock. There she was, the girl from the Disney World trip. My intuition was right. Going into crazy mode, I went swinging my fist all over the place. Yes I was ready to fight him and her. My best friend at the time kept holding me back, yelling, don't hit the girl, she looks young. Who cares? I told her, She in here with my man. That's when I came to my senses and realized he was not worth it. So I went home. That was my first real relationship, and it ended badly.

This was the start to bad relationships for me—getting cheated on seemed to start a bad pattern for me. Remember, I told you I didn't know how to be in a relationship, and it took me many years to figure it out. You're still young, people would say. Don't give up that easy, I was told. Who wants to get their heart broken? is what I told them. But I hadn't really experienced a real relationship yet.

Are all the guys that bad? Are all men horrible, or are they egotistical jerks? Why do they think that it's all about them? I'm not sure if I wanted to keep dating to find out. From now on, it will be all about me and not them, is what I told myself. But could I live up to the tough-hearted girl, or was I too weak not to know any better? All I wanted to do was live where there was complete happiness, and I was treated like a queen. Maybe that just doesn't exist in this world, but who knows. Maybe I'm wrong; maybe there will be someone waiting to sweep me off my feet. Everyone I meet is bringing me pain. Or is it me? Never will I go backwards, and I will always forgive.

Not letting men get too close to me was the plan. Trusting them was not an option. There was no such thing as putting my trust in a man. When I put trust in men, they hurt me. Trusting someone was left back in my past when my innocence was taken away from me. Sometimes I wished I would have stayed a virgin, and then life would have possibly been easy. I felt like I was just giving myself away with no purpose or meaning, just to feel wanted. But it was too late for that. I could only move forward and try to do things the right way.

The beginning of a lost child, teenager, and now woman. No guidance from a male figure, so who was I going to turn to? God. Yes, I knew about praying. I even carried a Bible in my purse, but did I believe or even have faith? Not at all. Having no faith and no patience at all made me feel so lost. Lost in a world where no one was kind. Thank God for music; it was still my escape. It helped me through my trying times in life. I can remember just being angry, and when I turned on those tunes, everything went away like nothing ever happened.

One of my favorite instruments was the saxophone, and I loved listening to jazz music. That was my peace away from this crazy, hurtful world. I had no thoughts because those horrible ones were still locked away. Never did I imagine that I would go through so much pain. I just knew my life was going to be a fairy tale when it came down to dating because I was such a nice person. But I guess being nice got me the short end of the stick. It gets worse before it gets better, is what I told myself. At times I had to give myself pep talks to keep moving throughout the day. I was so ready for better. Praying was all I had even though I didn't know how. I just put things together and tried to make sense of it. No matter what I was going through, I always talked to God. Maybe he would hear me one day or maybe he wouldn't. But at that time I really didn't think he was listening to me. At least he knows my heart.

Let's Give It Another Try

As time moved on, so did I. We moved to another new neighborhood, which meant new beginnings, and I was still living with my mom at the age of twenty-one. Why me? I seemed to be stuck with her. I couldn't keep a job to even get my own place, and I didn't even have a car even though I knew how to drive. Feeling a little low as usual I came across someone that I think I was crushing on. Looking like a creep, I used to watch him walk up and down the street. I think he started to notice me looking at him so he decided to talk to me. Conversation with him was great, but in the back of mind, I thought, he's probably not a good man either. He knew that I braided hair, so he let me do his. I didn't care because all I wanted was to be in his presence. He made me feel special and wanted. That was my weakness, just wanting to feel loved.

Fast forwarding a little, things got heavy between us. One thing led to another, and I was pregnant. Yes, I said it--pregnant. My first pregnancy ever. I didn't know what to think or do. I didn't have anything valuable to my name; how was

I going to take care of a baby? It happened so fast. I don't think he was truly ready, and his absence proved that to me. The distance from him started to come into play. I really didn't think he would turn out to be like this. Not the man that I was crushing on and sold me hopes and dreams. What is your problem? I asked him. He told me his grandmother had a dream that the baby was not his. I told him I don't sleep around with anyone, so yes, this baby was his. All I could do was scream and cry. Bad luck just followed me wherever I went. I told him to stay away if he wanted to and that's what he did. I was stressed out; nothing would ever go right for me. I didn't want a pity party; I just wanted something to go right for once.

Sucking it up like always and moving on is what I did, but I guess God had other plans, because I had a miscarriage. I was devastated, but I'm guessing he was happy since he wasn't ready anyway. I didn't want him near me. Maybe it's for the best because I wanted the best for me. No one should ever have to experience that. It's not good mentally or physically. And to go through it alone was the rough part. I did have my mother, but there's nothing like a companion to help you through, especially the one that helped with making the baby. Even though I went through that pain, I did not let it get me down too long. I had to move on like always. Just take this and add it to my chamber of thoughts, and one day all of it will be out in a book or in a movie. My story would be hurtful but helpful to some people, is what I thought. On the other hand, maybe I should just keep them locked away because no one really cares. As long as I had God on my side, he would guide me.

Two years passed and so did my feelings toward some people. I never looked back at the old relationships and problems. At this point in my life, I blocked out everything that caused me pain in any way. The molestation, watching my mom go through abuse, down to just being poor growing up. Having fun in my twenties was all I could think about at the time. Thoughts, painful thoughts, were locked away in a chamber inside of my brain. It was to the point I almost forgot they existed. Eventually, they would all reveal themselves in a storm full of emotions.

Let the Fun Begin

I had a fascination with motorcycles. Riding is what I loved to do, so I started to become a part of that world, hanging out, having tons of fun. Not an ounce of stress in me, just living. Having fun on this particular summer night, I came across this gentleman that I knew for a very long time. He was older than me and seemed very mature for his age, or at least I thought. We hit it off very well, and he liked the fact that I rode motorcycles. Date after date I just knew he was the one for me. He used to say all the right things, and I was so naïve to sweet talk. Falling for him so deeply was what I wanted to do, and I did. Not knowing that the great beginning was soon to come to an end.

Him being older charmed me right into getting pregnant. The first thought that came to my head was if I were able to carry the baby without a miscarriage. It felt so right in the beginning, knowing that I got a second chance at being a mom. Knowing that scared the hell out of me. I did not know what I was going to do, keep the baby or get rid of it. Bad thoughts I know, but that was the way of my life. I could not believe he was no help to me. He had mixed emotions as well. In the back of my head, I wanted to keep the baby because I always wanted a little boy, and I just had a feeling it was going to be one.

My mom had four girls. I knew how I was when I was growing up, and I just did not want the same for my child. I really didn't want anyone to take advantage of her as a child like someone did to me. One moment he wanted the baby, and the next moment he didn't. I was tired of playing these mind games with men. When will the right man come along and whisk me off my feet? I knew then that was not going to be him.

Pregnancy for me was not good in the beginning. I couldn't keep food down, I quit my job, and on top of that, being three-months pregnant, I had to dump the sperm donor. He decided he wanted nothing to do with the baby at all. He did what many immature men did--disappeared. All I could think about was why me. What did I do to deserve so much pain? I am the sweetest person that you could ever meet. Yes, I had my difficulties like everyone else, but why hurt me in a way I would never forget? Maybe I should just get rid of the baby since he does not want it, because I sure did not want to be a single mom. The tears began to fall. I had not cried like that in many years. This pain hurt so badly. The pain of abandonment was filling in my heart.

For many years, I always felt as if something was missing, and it was. The feeling of love was lost. Where would I find it? Who would give it to me? How would I know it was real or true? Someone please rescue me from it all. I am twenty-three, and I am still lost in a world where there has been no love for me, or at least that is what I was feeling. Feeling like love was all I needed but I didn't have a clue on what I needed because I didn't even love myself.

Let's get it together because my first child was on his way. The one person that did stick by my side was my mom, and to this day, I owe her the world, even if my childhood was not a good one for me. The Bible says honor thy mother and thy father and have everlasting days. So honoring her is what I was going to do. Still, in my heart, I resented many things that happened back then with her, but maybe one day I would find it in my heart to forgive her.

It was giving birth time. My stubborn baby was four days late. He was supposed to arrive September 16, 2006; instead, he came September 20, 2006, two days after my birthday. Yes, it was a boy. God did bless me with the one thing that I prayed for. We are both Virgos. What fun that was going to be? It was 3:00 a.m., and I thought I had to use the bathroom, but that was not the case at all.

The pain just kept coming so I knew it was time to go to the hospital. My neighbor gave my mom and me a ride down there. Once I got there, I was only dilated three centimeters, and the doctors told me to walk around to at least get to four so they could admit me. However, the pains were so bad I could not do so at all.

The time had come for me to push him out. No sperm donor in sight, but at least I had this fine anesthesiologist to help me out with my labor. I swear I would never forget those light brown eyes looking down holding my neck telling me to push. God must have sent him to my side to help me out, and I was not mad at him. Laughing to myself, I am thinking this is what got me into this position in the first place. I went to the hospital at three in the morning and didn't have him until 6:56 p.m. Such a long labor for me. So glad it was all over with, but why did I feel so sad? Why did I not feel a connection? Welcome to this world, Jadon Anthony Wilson. Six pounds and 7.5 ounces, my blessing from God.

Motherhood

As time passed, Jadon was growing fast, with no father in his life, but I knew we were going to be just fine. Better he stay away then to get on my nerves. Never knew why I kept getting the wrong batch of men. Maybe I was picking the wrong ones. Hey, I had to keep pushing no matter what; I had someone looking up to me. I thought, maybe I should just give up on men loving me the right way when I do not even love myself.

Months passed, and I did not hear anything from Jadon's father. I thought, maybe I should just give up, but the other side of me was going to let him know that he had to help raise our son. Being a single mom is very challenging. No woman should go through this. The one thing I did do on a daily basis was to keep God first. Some days I felt as if I was going crazy. Postpartum depression started to set in, but I had to shake those feelings off. I couldn't do this by myself, because it takes two to make a baby.

The Images of Me

Jadon turned two, and I sure could have used help. I so needed a break. I was frustrated and confused. I thought, I will start having a little fun, so I started leaving him home with my mom. Starting not to care anymore. This being a mom thing was taking a toll on me at the time. Waking up frustrated and depressed made me not care anymore. Yes, I loved my son, but I did not think I could be that much of a good mom to him. I struggled daily with giving him unconditional love. I really did not see harm in leaving him home to go have some fun for once. Hey, all I used to do with my sisters was babysit. I felt like I never got a real childhood because I had to grow up too fast. Sounds wrong, because at the end of the day, that was my child and not hers. I just did not care. Hanging out is what I wanted to do, so hanging out is what I did.

Feeling like a bad mom, I was always on the go. I took my son places, but I more so left him in the house with my mom. Some days I went too far and stayed out all night long. Somebody needed to give me an intervention, but I don't think that would have really helped at the time because I did not care. The resentment I had stored up in me was bad. I believed everybody else should take care of him instead of me. I felt like they owed me my sanity. If I was taught how to love as a child, when I first had him, maybe I would have showed him that love instead of running away. There goes that abandonment feeling.

My mom did not owe me anything, but in the back of my mind I felt like she did. Just make me over, put me in a different setting of life so I can do better. Who will listen, and whom can I turn to? I was holding so much inside, I did not even know how to deal with everyday life. No one truly knew my pain but me because I never shared anything with anyone. I said to myself, things will get better, and I promised I would take care of him forever and love him like I was supposed to be loved.

Let's Try Dating Again

My dating life was very bad to begin with. I sabotaged my own relationships, the worst part of me. Trying to date was not my biggest accomplishment since I did not trust men at all. Having no trust from the start with them made everything turn out to be so bad. I just did not know how to relax nor did I have any patience. Naïve and too nice to people is what I was. Getting a guy was not the hard part at all. It was keeping their attention long enough for them to want me as their girlfriend.

Growing up in my twenties and dating was challenging. As I'm sitting here now at the age of thirty-two, I sit back, shake my head, and laugh at the things that I went through. Because at the end of the day, it was my way or no way, and a lot of men do not put up with that. Either you did the things that I required or you just left me alone. And what guys love to do is leave. There was also that fear of abandonment. I was so afraid of getting into something and then getting my feelings hurt. As much as I loved someone, they always found a way to hurt me.

The Images of Me

Sometimes I wished I never wore my feelings on my sleeve and wished it wasn't so easy for me to fall in love with someone. I was just the girl that wanted to be loved. The feeling of not having love made me chase it at any given second. I just wanted to be wanted. Most of the time, when I did chase and look for love, I always ended up with not so good people. Some people weren't bad, it was just I was too much into them for them to want something serious with me. I was just this young woman, trapped, looking for love in the wrong places; a young woman feeling the love lost because her dad left at an early age. I just wanted someone to replace the love that I was missing. I was strong on the outside but weak and broken on the inside, waiting for someone to come along and put my puzzle pieces together. It would be challenging, but it would make sense and be perfect one day.

Suppressing all my feelings from the past and present made things complicated with dating. There goes that trust again that made everything so complicated. "Maybe I just don't love myself." That was it. I never really saw the beauty in me. I hated myself. Everything about me. I didn't think I was pretty enough or good enough for anyone. Who was going to love me? Numb is how I felt the majority of my life. Numb to life and the world. What if I was gone? Who would miss me? I tried not to think like that because I had a son to live for. Who was going to provide for him better than me, his mom?

Giving away what God gave to me was not what he wanted at all. The attraction from men because of this coke-bottle shape he gave me was beginning to be a bit too much. I wanted someone to look past that and accept me for the nice, kind, beautiful person that I am. Was that too much to ask? Will I ever be rescued by my king or will I be a lonely old lady who won't grow old with anyone? Maybe that was just a fairy tale. Since I'm a Virgo, I'm something like a perfectionist, trying to plan everything out, knowing damn well it would not work that way. Lord just don't let me grow old without him, is what I used to say.

Opening Up and Letting Go

My life was a complete mess at this point. So much time had passed, so many good and bad things had gone on in my life. On top of that, it was time to kick open thirties' door. Was I ready? Oh no, not at all. No career, no amazing job, still living at my mom's house feeling stuck. In shock because I couldn't really believe I was turning thirty and had nothing to show for it. I was so hard on myself because I wanted the best for me and my son, and I felt as if I had failed by chasing love. Where did my twenties go, and why did I waste so much time?

As soon as I turned thirty, the depression and sadness made its way back into my life. The chamber was finally reaching its breaking point. Maybe it was too full of hurt and pain and needed to be released. I wasn't sure if I was ready to release any of it. That would mean opening up and sharing my thoughts and secrets. My best friend at the time, Tynisha, told me to sit down and talk to someone so that I wouldn't be down and out anymore. Even though she was younger than me she always looked out for my best interest. Me running to her for advice all the time, she never turned her back on me, and I still look up to her to this day. She's one of my biggest motivations. (Love ya girl.) Anywho, let's get back to the story. I was not sure if I was ready to tell my secret since no one knew what was hurting me all these years. Feeling so helpless and talking to God was so easy at this point. He was the only one that truly knew my pain. He kept me through it all.

Every day I prayed, even though some days I didn't think he was listening at all. That was the negative thinking that stayed with me through many years of growing up. I was in the midst of this storm, and I knew I had to find a way to get out of it, but little did I know I had to go through it. Not knowing how long it would take was the scary part. I was tired of waking up depressed and sad. I had to do something about it. So to church I went. I joined my Church Empowerment Temple, where the best pastor I know resides. On this particular Sunday that I went, the pastor made an altar call about releasing the past. My heart stopped--it was my time--time to let go of all the shame and hurt. He introduced someone by the name of Candice, and she was a sexual abuse counselor. I immediately signed up after service because I was ready. God sent me there to receive the message, so I had to do my part and talk to her.

It was time for the session. I was nervous. What was I thinking, coming here? I'm not ready to tell all. How would I begin? I saw this type of thing happen in the movies. Meeting her was the best day of my life. Crying every session was a joy of relief. I did not know how much hurt and pain I was holding on to. She allowed me to talk when I finally stopped the tears. Letting everything out was truly a blessing. So much hate and disturbance was leaving my body. The toxic childhood, baring all that pain, was too much for me, but it had to be done. It was time to be happy again--truly happy. Finding peace within myself and giving up what was holding me back was going to be a challenge. But with God on my side I knew it would be done one day. It wouldn't be easy because nothing in life ever came easy for me. There was always hard work to be done. I had to start with forgiveness. First, I had to forgive my mom and dad in my heart in order to move on with life.

I'm grown now, so I have to answer to God for myself and my son. Struggling day to day with everything was not easy. I believe God challenges us in many ways. He doesn't want us to ever fail. When things seem to get rough, he wants us to turn to him; even on our good days, just say thank you. Let him know that you're there and you just don't need him when things aren't good.

I was going through my storm for two years. Remember it hit me when I was thirty, and I'm thirty-two now. Let me tell you, it was rough. There were times I just wanted to give in and not go on, but looking at my son and praying to God didn't allow me to fail. You have to find that peaceful place within yourself or somewhere you can go just to release the anger because it will only make things worse if you don't let go of that painful past. Believe me, I'm not perfect, and he is still working on me. Again, that phrase comes to mind: "Thank God I don't look like what I been through." I live by those words. If people could really just judge me from the outside, they probably would say she's well put together. And I would say, not this girl from the hood; it took me a long time to get to this place of peace that I'm in, and I can't stop thanking God for bringing me out of that storm and giving me this vision to empower women to be better and to let go of the past.

In order to move forward and heal, you have to go through it. Reach out and talk to someone; let them be a guidance for you. I promise, you won't fail and be disappointed with your outcome. As I was growing up, I felt as If I didn't have that one person that I could talk to or open up to. Granted, many people crossed my path but not for me to share anything with them. It wasn't until God led me to meet Angela Wharton, whom I consider my mentor and sister in Christ. There were days when I couldn't move forward or continue throughout the day. I would call her on the phone and share with her what I was feeling; even when I was in tears, she would understand and immediately pray for me. Angela would be at work at the time, but that didn't bother her because she was there if I needed a listening ear. I thank God for her and for her helping a woman like me to overcome everything that I was going through.

Writing this book really helped me put an end to the hurt and pain. I once came across a guy who told me that I can't use my past as a crutch, and at first I was like, he doesn't know what I've been through, how could he tell me anything? But as I look back at my past, smiling at my present, and excited about my future, I would tell him he was absolutely right. So I thank him for coming into my life and helping me to let go of what I couldn't change, because it does not define the person I am today. I'm at peace, and I don't allow negativity to reside near me. I'm living for God, my son, and myself.

Peace

and

Blessings

Peace of Mind

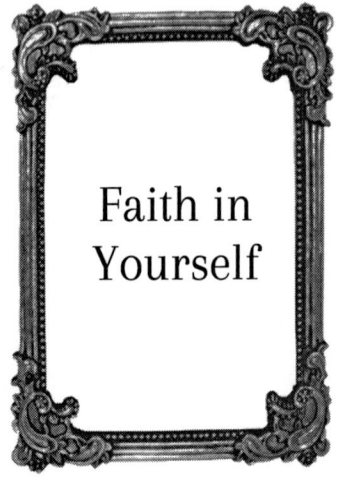

Forgiveness

Purpose

Faith in Yourself

How to Heal

Heal me, Lord, and I will be healed; save me and I will be saved, for you are the one I praise.

Jeremiah 17:14 NIV

The one thing I have learned at this point is that you will never be at your full potential if you do not allow yourself to heal. Healing means to let go of whatever is troubling you or hurting you on the inside. It first starts with opening up and talking about things. I remember when I did not want to say a word to anyone, but each and every day, I was silently suffering from the pain. It took me many years to finally say to myself that I needed help.

Sometimes, I wish while growing up in my twenties that I had that one person to rescue me and help me release everything I was going through, instead of holding on to the pain for so many years and enduring so many trials and tribulations. The most important thing in life is learning how to heal yourself.

Beautiful You Are

Charm is deceptive, and beauty is fleeting; but a woman who fears the Lord is to be praised.

Proverbs 31:30

My child, you are beautiful, and let no one ever tell you that you are not. Growing up, I struggled with myself. I did not think I was pretty at all. The ugly duckling is what I called myself. Perhaps the black sheep of the family. Everyone was lighter than I was, and here I come a shade darker. My aunt always told me I was pretty, and at a young age I told myself that, but as I got older and saw other people prettier than me, that's when the low self-esteem kicked in. I looked for others to tell me I was beautiful and did not even believe what they were saying. I could not even look in the mirror too long because I did not see myself, until one day I got tired of feeling so low about myself, I looked into that mirror and uttered the words, you are beautiful and you are loved.

From that day forward I repeated it over and over; even if it was a challenge, I did it anyway. Now I go through life knowing and feeling beautiful. So when someone other than myself tells me that, I can say thank you with greatness in my heart.

Self-Love/Love Thyself

So now faith, hope, and love abide, these three; but the greatest of these is love.

1 Corinthians 13:13 ESV

Let us talk about the one most important thing in life to deal with--loving yourself. First and foremost, how can you not love the beautiful person that God created? We were made in his image. I too struggled with loving myself. In fact, I hated myself. I never seemed to be able to accomplish anything that I started. I always gave up at the first sight, until one day I decided to love me. I asked myself, how would anybody truly love me if I didn't love myself? No one will love you like you. So you must first find out why you don't love yourself and what happened along the way to make you feel like that. The worst part about not loving yourself is always feeling lost or always feeling like you're missing something. Don't keep going through life without self-love. It will save you a lifetime full of pain.

Know Your Worth

Rather, it should be that of your inner self, the unfading beauty of a gentle and quiet spirit, which is of great worth in God's sight.

1 Peter 3:4 NIV

We must know that we're worthy to do and be anything that we want. God gave us the ability to become the best. And the best is what we should give him, while praising and worshiping him. We all fall short of his glory, but he will never forsake us. When knowing your worth shows its full potential, the old person who could not see its true beauty will no longer exist. I was once stuck in a world where I didn't think I was good enough for true love, until God put something in me that woke up the inner beauty that had been hiding for so long. Now I can see far beyond my worth, and I won't settle for less. Dig deep and pray every day that God restores your worthiness.

Peace of Mind

Peace I leave with you; my peace I give you. I do not give to you as the world gives. Do not let your hearts be troubled and do not be afraid.

John 14:27

This scripture was well said. God did not give us fear. He gave us faith to believe in him and believe that no matter what he sets upon us, we will never fail. Failure is not an option when we have God by our side. For many years, I felt as if my mind was racing nonstop. The negative thinking took over my entire life, which allowed me to live in fear every day. Some days I did not know where I was going. Other days I would feel like I was on track, and then in a moment, I was lost again. I was always searching for that peace of mind. Little did I know, having that meant releasing my past. When that time came to let it go, I felt a big burden lift off my shoulders. The best feeling in the world is to have a stress-free peace of mind.

Purpose

And we know that in all things God works for the good of those who love him, who have been called according to his purpose.

Romans 8:28

Everyone has a purpose here on earth. No one is promised the next day. If we live by God's word, our days can be longer. For many years, I did many things without prayer. No faith is what I had, and no patience at all. I lived in the moment with many regrets. When my prayer life began, I really hoped to find what I was truly brought on this earth to do. When God gives you a vision and a purpose to fulfill, nothing or no one will be able to stop you. Even if you don't feel like pursuing that dream, he will store a fire inside of you that won't keep you still until you live out that vision he gave you.

Truth Be Told

Truth be told, no one will treat you better than yourself. Take a day where you have what I call "me time." Me time is when you can look back and reflect on your great accomplishments. Thank God for your trials and tribulations. They are what make us stronger in life. That is when the truth will set you free. When you're true to being who you are, no one can come against you and bring forth harm. The way we live our lives is based on how we carry ourselves as individuals. I've struggled for so many years to set a goal for myself and stick to it. I gave up on so many dreams.

Battling with the fact that I didn't feel loved at all made me make bad choices in life. When you can't keep a job, it takes a toll on your life. However, today I choose to follow my heart and stick with what I love to do. So stay true to who you are and follow your heart in what you want to be in life.

Afraid to Love

Have you ever been so afraid of love that you ran from it?

Have you ever been so afraid of love that you sabotaged it?

Being afraid to love is what I went through in my twenties.

I've always expected it to be so perfect, that if I gave it a try, it would not turn out to be so nice.

I never allowed love to fully grab ahold of me,

Feeling like love from a person was just to hurt me.

Never did I want to give anyone a chance, but one day while praying, I learned that it was time to Just let go of hurtful love and allow real love to find me.

So never block love, because that person that God's sent is waiting to love you the real way.

Imperfect You

Being imperfect means you don't have it all together. Me, I lived in this imperfect world trying to be perfect all the time, failing at many obstacles and being so hard on myself. Why must I have been so imperfect? I just wanted to have a perfect life, where nothing ever went wrong. No one is perfect, is what someone once told me. We will have failure after failure, but it's getting back up that makes it worth it. Getting back up that makes us stronger. We live in an imperfect world being imperfect people trying to serve a perfect God.

You Are Queens

Dear queens, value your worth. I grew up not knowing what that word stood for. Who was going to teach me how to be a queen? Feeling unworthy of myself and not seeing the beauty in me made me feel less than a queen. Queens are supposed to stand strong in faith, and faith is what I prayed for over and over. At this point of my life, I know that I'm a strong, black queen. I stand strong in faith every day. I'm here to empower women on a daily basis to embrace the queen that lives inside of them and to encourage them to let their inner light shine bright.

Forgiveness

Forgive your hurt

Forgive your past

Forgive those that caused harm to you

Forgiveness means letting things go

Trust the process

Forgive yourself

Trust and believe everything will be okay

Have faith in God

Have faith in yourself

Give without looking for something in return

Just remember to trust the process. That process will not be easy. There will be times you just want to give up on being better because being the broken person is much easier. But trust me, when you allow God to lead you, the healed you will be so much better, and you will know it was all worth the tears and pain.

Determination

Be determined to finish what you start

Determination means to never give up at the first sight of failure

Procrastination will stop you from becoming your full, potential self in life

Determine to be great

Determine to be healthy

Encourage others

Use your gift of wisdom to bless others

Speak life in your vision or purpose

Speak life into others

About the Author

Tamara McKnight has a passion for empowering women to motivate, love, and respect each other. Her mission is to save a soul, as God has saved hers, by spreading her story and guiding others to find peace within themselves. Tamara believes that once we learn to love ourselves, we will be able to grow into the women that God has created us to be.

Along with writing, Tamara loves being a mom to her son, Jadon, and riding motorcycles in her hometown of Baltimore, Maryland.

To connect with Tamara, please visit:
www.theimageofme1983.com

purposely created
PUBLISHING

WE WANT TO HEAR FROM YOU!!!

If this book has made a difference in your life Tamara would be delighted to hear about it.

Leave a review on Amazon.com!

BOOK TAMARA TO SPEAK AT YOUR NEXT EVENT!

Send an email to: booking@publishyourgift.com
Learn more about Tamara at:
www.TheImageOfMe1983.com

FOLLOW TAMARA ON SOCIAL MEDIA

TheImageOfMe   TamaraMcKnight

"EMPOWERING YOU TO IMPACT GENERATIONS"
WWW.PUBLISHYOURGIFT.COM

CPSIA information can be obtained
at www.ICGtesting.com
Printed in the USA
LVOW10s1624240717
542442LV00016B/865/P

9 781945 558030